AF427534

MANCHESTER
18   94
CITY

DE BRUYNE
17

INTRODUCTION

Manchester City has seen several peaks throughout its vibrant lifetime, much like its rivals in Mancun. The town stands as one of most successful English football clubs ever, with First Division/Premier League titles, FA Cups, League Cups and one Cup Winners' Cup. Yet their past has more than enough downs to it; for instance, City is still the only English champions to be relegated to the next season.

The 1904 FA Cup champs' team.

History

In 1880, the club was founded by Arthur Connell (The Rector of St. Mary's Church) and its daughter, Anna Connell, under the name of St. Mark's.

After branding them the Gorton FC and Ardwick AFC, they changed their names in 1894 to Manchester City. The outcome is some financial difficulties which ultimately resulted in the club's restructuring. Combined with the change in the name, Manchester

City was turned into a very spacious grounds a few years later and the loyal fan base followed them everywhere they went. The increase in stature contributed to the first division being promoted in 1899

Shortly after City won its first FA Cup in 1904, 17 of their players were suspended on charges of financial fraud, which led Billy Meredith, a club star player, to transfer across town to United, where he won a two-league title later. In 1923, due to a fire that demolished the main stand of Hyde Road, the club relocated into Maine Road.

In 1934, by winning their second FA Cup, City was back on the road to success. In one game – which stands today – the club broke a record for the largest number of participants with 84,566 home fans on Maine Road for the 6th-round match against Stoke CityThree years later, City took over a trophy in style in the first division and scored more than 100 objectives during the season. However, the next season, the first time a defending champion team was demoted, they were relegated.

Decline

A long period of decline followed. It is high time for improvement with only one FA Cup over the next three decades, and attendance steadily declines. After Joe Mercer was appointed manager in 1965, the club went on a hot line; City won both the English Cup and a Cup Winner's Cup titles during its six years of leadership. The club won another League Cup in 1976 after the Mercer era before succumbing to another lengthy spell of mediocrity.

In England, the return to top soccer began in the 1998-99 season.

City managed to climb from the second division to the first division after an amazing play-off match against Gillingham. The team succeeded in going to the Premier directly via Division 1. After the Premier League relegation, they will win the First Division 10 points ahead of West Bromwich in the next season. And then Manchester City formed them as a Premier League team.

Maine Road has been the home stadium of City for many years, but in 2003 the City of Manchester stadium with a much larger capacity was completed.

PART ONE

<u>WHEN THE JOURNEY STARTED</u>

The Football Curve

The football club, known as Manchester City, was established for primarily charitable purposes by the Founders of St. Marks's Church of England (West Gorton, Manchester). Two church guards tried to reduce local gang violence and alcoholism by creating new activities for local men, while East Manchester, particularly Gorton, suffered high unemployment. All men, regardless of religion, were invited to enter.

In 1875, there was a cricket club in the church, although no counterpart had existed for the winter months. The church leaders William Beastow and Thomas Goodbehere started in the winter of 1880 a team of church football players called the St Mark's (West Gorton) (sometimes written as the West Gortons (St Marks)), to rectify this and as a part of Rector Arthur Connell's general pushing for action in social ills.

The first match recorded by Team was against a Macclesfield team on 13 November 1880. St. Marks lost the game 2-1, winning just one game in his opening season 1880-81, and in March 1881, winning Staly Bridge.

By winning the Second Division in 1899, city won its first prize; the First Division, which became its highest level in English football. The first major honors were claimed in 1904 on April 23, 1904 and the Bolton Wanderer was beaten 1–0 in the Crystal Palace for winning the FA cup. After finishing in the League, the city lost a League and Cup twice in that saison, but City was Manchester's first major club.

The club was exposed to financial irregularities in the seasons following the victory of the FA Cup and resulted in the suspension in 1906 of seven players, including Captain Billy Meredith, who subsequently crossed the city to Manchester United. A fire at Hyde Road destroyed the main booth in 1920 and in 1923, at Maine Road on Moss Side, the club relocated to their newly-built Stadium.

Manchester City F.C. (1928–1965)

Manchester City reached two consecutive finals at the FA Cup in the 1930's and lost Everton in 1933 before winning the Cup in 1934, when it defeated Portsmouth. During the 1934 Cup Race, Manchester City smashed the record for any club's top hometowning in the history of English football, when 84,569 Maine Road enthusiasts wrestled with Stoke City for a sixth round of the FA Cup in 1934. The Club won the first Division title in 1937, although it scored more goals than any other divisional team the next season was relegated.

Twenty years later, in 1955 and 1956, another consecutive FA Cup final met a City team based on a tactical system known as the Revie Plan; just as during the 30's they lost the first to Newcastle United and won the second. The 1956 finale, during which Manchester City defeated Birmingham City 3–1, is one of the world-renowned finals. Bert Trautmann, the town's goalkeeper, is well known for continuing despite having broken his neck unequivocally.

Manchester City F.C. (1965–2001)

The future looked grim with record low house participation by 8,015 in January 1965 against Swindon Town after being relegated to the second division in 1963. The Joe Mercer and Malcolm Allison management team was named in the Summer of 1965. In Mercer's first time, City won the title of the Second Division and won important signatures in Colin Bell and Mike Summerbee. Two seasons later, Manchester City won the League Championship for the second time in 1967–68, won 4–3 at Newcastle United on the final day of season, beating Manchester United's near-by neighbors second. There followed other trophies:

City went on to win the FA Cup in 1969 and the European Winners Cup in 1970 won Górnik Zabrze in Vienna before achieving European success. In the same season, City won the League Cup and became the second English team that won a European trophy and a national trophy.

The club managed to compete for honors in the 1970s, complete two times one point behind the league champions and end the 1974 League Cup final. One of the matches that Manchester's supporters recall most is the final match of the 1973–74 season against the Manchester United archrival, which needed to win to prevent relegation.

Former United player Denis law scored a 1-0 victory in Old Trafford with a backheel to confirm his rivals' relegation. In 1976, Newcastle

United won the final Trophy for the most prosperous time of the club, as the League Finals went on to defeat 2-1.

The success of the 1960s and 1970s was accompanied by a long decrease. Malcolm Allison joined the club for the second time in 1979, but spent significant amounts on insufficient signatures, such as Steve Daley. There followed a number of managers – 7 alone in the 1980's.

The city reached the final of the 1981 FA Cup, under John Bond, but lost in Tottenham Hotspur's return. In 1983 and 1987 the club was two times relegated from top flight, but again in 1989 it was fifth under Peter Reid's leadership in 1991 and 1992. This was, however, a temporary break and the fortunes of Reid began to decline after he left Manchester City. After its formation in 1992, City was the cofounder of the Premier League, and after the first ninth season, three seasons of fighting were experienced before it was relegated in 1996.

After two seasons in Division One, City came into the lowest point in its history, after being relegated to the third league level in their country as the second European trophy winner. German FC Magdeburg.

Manchester City F.C. (2001–present)

After relegation, the club faced a revolt from outside, with the introduction of more fiscal discipline by new chairman David Bernstein.. In the first attempt, a play-off against Gillingham was promoted in Area, dramatically. The second successive promotion saw the return to the top division of City, but it proved to be a step too far for the recovery club. In the close season Kevin Keegan arrived as the new boss, returning to the top of the team immediately as the club won the 2001-02 championship, breaking records of the number of points won by the club and scored goals during one season..

The 2002-03 season was the last on Maine Road and saw a 3–1 derby win over Manchester United's rivals, finishing 13 years without a derby victory. For the first time in 25 years, City was also entitled to the European competition. The club moved to Manchester Stadium in 2003. During the close season. All had midtable finish in the first four seasons of the stadium. Former manager in England Sven-Göran Eriksson was hired in 2007 to be the first manager for the club from abroad. In the second half of the season, after a bright initial display, Eriksson was sacked in June 2008. Two days later on 4 June 2008, Eriksson was replaced by Mark Hughes.

The club stood in a difficult financial condition by 2008. Some year ago, Thaksin Shinawatra had taken over the club, but his political works had frozen his assets. Afterwards, the Abu Dhabi United Group bought the club in August 2008. The purchase was quickly followed by a flourish of offers to high-profile actors; the club broke the British record by signing Real Madrid's Brazilian International Robinho for £32.5 million. However, the results of the previous season were not much better, although they did well to reach the quarter finals of the UEFA cup despite the influx of funds, finishing tenth for the side.

The Club invested more than 100 million pounds on players Gareth Barry, Roque Santa Cruz, Kolo Touré, Emmanuel Adebayor, Carlos Tevez and Joleon Lescotz, and move to an unparalleled amount in the summer of 2009. In December 2009, Roberto Mancini succeeded him as chairman, Mark Hughes – who was hired shortly before the change of business but initially retained the current board. Two years later City finished fifth, just missing a place in the Champions League, and in the 2010–11 season City qualified for the UEFA Europa League.

Players' interest continued in progressive seasons, and player quality outcomes began to be co-ordinated. In the first important last year, City reached the 2011 FA Cup Last in over thirty years, the first time they took their opponent out of the cup rivalries since 1975 after overthrowing derby competitors in Manchester. Stir up City 1–0 was won last and their Fifth FA Cup was the first meaningful trophy since the Alliance Cup was won in 1976. Since 1968, the club, which was fitted with a 1-0 chief class for the UEFA Champions Division, has dominated Tottenham Hotspur in the same week.

On the last day of the 2010-2011 season, town surpassed its arsenal and thus won third position on the league stage. The 2011–2012 season started with solid results and the club took the lead from the following season: 5–1 in the white hart line, 5–1, 6–1 in the united stadium, and the humbling manchester..

Although its solid shape went down 1/2 way over the season and at one point metropolis dropped behind its competitive competitors by 8 factors with 6 easy videospielen left for action, an exceptional drop by the previous champions allows the blue facet of the team to pull the stage off with two games at the front and set an exciting finale for each party in the rest of the season.

Despite the most successful metropolis that needed a national win against the team in the relegation zone, it still managed to fall into the rear of the intention by way of a standard split, mainly a number of United players who celebrated their recreation with the idea of winning the Championship. Desires in harmful times – such as one scored almost 5 minutes every day – finished in an almost-literal closing minute triumph, the first in 40 four years, and the fifth party was the handiest to win the most desirable league in 1992.

Under the ensuing series, the potential was described by the United Kingdom media and the industry, since the biggest moment in the most select ligue records. For a former athlete Joey Barton the sport became all the more unbelievable, when he committed three different purple card-able incidents in just a few seconds on three exclusive players, resulting in a 12-game ban, which rightly forced him to quit English Food.

However, following the end of the season, which many thought would only spur City, some of the gains made in the first two full seasons of Mancini were not capitalized on

On the window of the move, almost no players joined the club until the last day of the season when four different players all joined in about 10 hours during a last minute explosion. The free flow of soccer in the past season was unusual and, while the City seldom seemed to collapse in the second position, it was a slight title challenge every season..

The team has been excluded from the UEFA Champions League for a second season at the group stage, confirming Mancini's credibility even stronger in domestic games than in Europe, although a second finale of the FA Cup in the third season ended in a 1–0 loss for Wigan Athletic. The loss resulted in the rejection of Mancini ostensibly because he had been unable to meet his goals for the season, but many in the press were implying a disintegration of relations between Mancini, his players, but also between Italians and the board superiors.

The Chilian Manuel Pellegrini was named in his place, and his Champions League record was much more impressive, but less respectable as an award-winner.

New triumphant era

A fresh, victorious period has been marked by the 2008 takeover by Abu Dhabi billionaire Sheik Mansour. Now one of the world's wealthiest clubs, City began to get busy on the transfer market immediately, recruiting several big-name signings for record fees. The club invested over £ 500 million on players in the five years since Mansour took over. The decision to change the name of the home stadium to Etihad Stadium in 2011 also exhibited the impact of Abu Dhabi.

Man City line up 2011 FA Cup final v. Stoke (1-0).

The club was reborn in its glory for the following years, winning Premier, an FA Cup and a League Cup titles. A highlight in the 2017-2018 season was the League win, as City became the first team ever to score 100 points in one year in the Premier Leagues. Town also made a new record for successive league wins (18).

The gap of 19 points from the first to the second team was entirely new to a league that was regarded as the most competitive in the game.

Logo

Three separate logos have been used by Manchester City. The first edition was discontinued in 1960, but again in use for a short time. In the second version, released in the 1960's, the 2016 logo replaced the eagle behind the shield used since 1997. The present logo is furnished with the ship (the symbol of the town's trading function) above and Red Rose of Lancaster at the bottom of the shield (the symbol of Lancashire's historical connection).

Football club of Manchester City was founded as St. Mark's in 1880 and in 1894 it took its current name.. The City of Manchester Stadium is currently home but has been at Maine Road until 2003.

Meaning and history

The iconic Manchester City FC, founded in 1880 as the St. Mark football club, had only been renamed in 1894, so that the original emblem of the famous FC had been designed for the team of a different name. Although from 1894 on, the club developed its visual identity only around Manchester's historic coat of arms.

The St. Mark's FC insignia consisted of a heavy circular monochrome, broad frame, made of a white double contour. There was a bold white Cross in the center of the symbol put on black, creating a stark contrast. The white wordmark — "St" was located between two circles of the badge outlines. Mark's West Gordon's was written around the border of the logo in all capitals of an easy

sans-serif typeface, halved by the date mark "1880" into two parts.

1894 — 2011

The club adopted an official Manchester coat with arms as its main

emblem after the establishment of Manchester City FC. And the key or additional insignia was this striking heraldic image until the beginning of the 2010s.

23

The armrest consisted of an orange shield with three oblique yellow lines. A clipper put on a white and blue background can be seen on the top of the shield. The shield stands on the green grass and is surrounded by birds, with a blue and pink blue, a white wild man to the right and a golden lion to the top and a globe.

The 1960s

The heraldic logo was introduced in the simplified version in the 1960s. This orange and yellow shield was mounted on a light-blue background surrounded by a thick circular frame of white and black with a black sans-shield inscription around its edge. The cutter was also rendered in yellow on this symbol and mounted on a white and orange base.

The logo was restructured in 1979. Every pattern has been altered and the colour, the structure of the light blue and the wordmark - gold in a black outline - turned into a more exciting colour. The shield was modernized, the principal part of the insignia, and now the lines were bolder, balanced and the clamper was mounted with wavy yellow lines on a white backdrop.

1972 — 1976

In 1972, there was a red rose on the shield to replace the diagonal lines. Now the gold screen was placed on the light blue background and featured a bold and massive sans-serif lettering around the perimeter of the white frame. The blue backdrop of the yellow clipper was tender and elegant.

1981 — 1997

In 1981 the tones of the emblem were enriched. The shield received

gradient blue and white tones, adding volume and elegance to the

symbol, and the inner circle was a little lighter than the previous

edition. The wordmark in the base of the frame remained untouched

and a strong black dot.

1997 — 2016

In 1997 the club again agreed to alter their logo. It was a revolutionary idea that the team embraced and remained with them for almost 20 years and is considered to be one of their most famous logos.

The blue shield was placed on the body of the golden eagle, whose head went to the left, with three white diagonals. There were three 5 point golden stars above the eagle, positioned to honor the winners and trophies of the club. Under the shield there was a white curved ribbon with the motto of the club in which the "Superbia In Proelio" was written in black in an old-tyle cursive.

As far as the crest itself is concerned, it has retained its key elements — strips and cutters, but they have now been cut by a bold black line with "M. C. F. C. "Serif gold abbreviation.

2016 — Today

In 2016 Manchester City agreed to restore the rounded badge with a red rose in the 1990s. On a double-blue and golden outline the shield featured the gold clipper, while on a blue striped background a red rose. The royal blue wordmark lies along the edge of the circular frame, which is done in a new, solid without serpent typeface. The date mark "1894" is horizontally mounted on the frame by means of a blue light.

The logo was updated to a brand new one in 1976. A chicken and a lion stood next to a shield with a red crown.

Below, the slogan "Concilio et labore" can be read. It was used for just five years, though, and in 1981 the team restored its old logo.

Current emblem

The 1997 logo was quite criticized by fans of the team, so it became natural for the club to change it less than ten years later. The club consulted with fans about what it could look like shortly before a new logo was set up.

At the end of 2015 the new logo was unveiled. It looks more like the older than the 1997 logo, in fact. Again, the familiar form is visible round. The image resembles somehow the logos of other City Football Community clubs. There is a shield indoors that houses a golden ship and the red Lancashire rose.

Font

In the latest edition of the Manchester City logo, the all-cap typeface

is without serif looks clear and minimalistic.

Color

The home colors of the team are light blue (often known as blue sky) and white. We can also note that the color palette of the remote kit consists of the maroon or a red-black combination. No information is available as to when and how these colors were selected. The only thing that is certain is that since 1892 or earlier blue has been used in football matches.

Manchester City FC timeline

The Club (named St. Mark's) was founded in 1880.

1887 Ardwick AFC is renamed the club.

1887 Moving the club into the stadium of Hyde Park.

The founding member of Division 2 is Ardwick AFC.

1893 The first foreign player for City and also for Football League is Canadian Walter Bowman.

1894 Manchester City is renamed the club.

1896 Participation in the First FA Cup.

1899 For the first time, the team will be promoted to Division 1.

1904 Secure their first trophy for the tournament (FA Cup).

1923 MCFC moved to stadium Main Route.

1937 Winners of Division 1 for the first time.

A new logo has been approved in 1965.

1970 Their first European competition (the Cup of Winners) was won.

In 1979, Steve Daley was the first player to have a fee of plus 1 million £ (£1,450,277) transferred to the club.

1997 There is a new logo.

2008 The new owner of the club is the Abu Dhabi United Group.

The first British double in 2014 (the League and the League Cup).

2015 Kevin De Bruyne becomes the first player to pay more than 50 million pounds (55 million pounds) in the club.

Manchester City Fc Nickname - The Citizens - Nickname History

The People call themselves Manchester City Fans. Many football clubs today in England are rooted in numerous church clubs, like Manchester City.

The Sent Marks Football Club was founded by members of the Southeastern Church of Manchester in the 1880s.

After numerous changes in club and playground names in 1894, the company was reorganized and the name was changed to Manchester City permanently.

The colors of Manchester City are blue and white. Paradise. The club has the Blue Jersey color, no clear response.

The origins of the blue and white colors of the home is also unknown, although the club is blue since 1892 or earlier.

In addition, there are photographic records from 1884 that depicts the team with a black jersey with a white cross that indicates the club's roots as a church team.

Manchester City First Kit

However, the new Manchester City Football Club logo is very different and most of them are known as The People.

The song of the City fans is a blue moon – many City fans even name the Blue Moon club.

There are few other niche names, all of which refer to the colors of the club—heavenly blues, sky blues or the simple and short city.

MANCHESTER CITY MOST SUCCESSFUL MANAGER - PEP GUARDIOLA

Pep Guardiola, who signed a three-year deal, has been appointed Manager of Manchester City on 1 February 2016.

Pep played a major role in Man City, making it possible for them to win the Premier League twice, three times in a row, and the FA Cup. The Community shield has also twice been awarded.

Under the management of Pep Guardiola, they won the Premier League in 2018 and in just one season have they earned 100 points.

Moonchester is a Blue Moon alien, who heard signals from a major football team, first of all to Maine Road then to Etihad Stadium.

Kit Manufacturer: Puma

In July 2019, Puma became Manchester City's technical kit provider

It has been released in the newspapers, making it the third biggest deal in English football. It was 50 million pounds a year.

Manchester City's Football League Wins

Manchester City won several league titles and also were runners up and champions each time they won promotion. Manchester City is also a winner.

Division First (now the Premier League)

> 1936/37, 1967/68 winners.

> The 1904, 1920/21, 1976/77, 2012/12. The 2014/15 runners-up are the first ones of their kind.

Division Two (now the Football League Championship)

> Champions 1898/99, 1902/03, 1909/10, 1926/28, 1965/66, 2001/02, Champions 1898/99.

1895/96, 1950/51, 198/89, and 1999/00

Division III (now Football League One)

1998/99 Play Off Champions

The FA Cup Wins of Manchester City

Manchester City won the FA Cup six times with a solid 6-0 win over Watford in 2019, with its latest triumph. Five years, the city was also a runner-up.

Manchester City Fan Club

Manchester City runs the free software Cityzen for its fans.

Citizens is a city fans family. You are a part of the Club when you enter and your loyalty is paid off.

FACTS ABOUT MANCHESTER CITY THAT MANY FANS MAT NOT KNOW

Manchester City goalkeeper John Burridge was the oldest player to have played in prime time. He was 43 years old, 4 months old and 26 days old when he substituted Manchester City v Newcastle United on April 29, 1995.

2. A significant portion of their squad was stopped due to financial fraud just a few years after Manchester City won the FA Cup in 1906. There is no awareness of the particulars of this case, but 17 players have been suspended, which greatly impairs the team's competition.

3. In 1937-38 it was the only club with a positive goal difference to ever be relegated with (80-77).

4. In the 1969 to 1970s, Man city won the most successful race: the FA Cup (1969), the European Cup Winners' Cup (1970) and the League Cup (1970).

5. The record of British transfer was held twice in Manchester City, with Robinho from Real Madrid in 2008 at £32.5 million in 1979, and once for steve daley in Wolverhampton wonderser in 1979.

6. Glyn Pardoe, 15 years 314 days in 1963 (compared to Birmingham City, First Division) was the youngest player ever in the city.

7. In 1904 City won its first FA cup.

8. In 1970, City won the Old Cup winners Cup under Joe Mercer, who later became the most outstanding and successful manager in City.

9. In 1957/58, Manchester city scored more than 100 goals just to give 100 goals that season.

10. 10. Manchester City has been known as Ardwick FC for the first seven years in its existence.

11. 11. Eric Brook is the greatest city ever.

Eric Brook is the highest scorer for the city with 178 goals at 494.

Manchester city Guardiola Tactics Overview

Pep Guardiola is certainly recalled as one of the best soccer coaches ever. Johan Cruyff's disciple, Pep is a crucial benchmark for aspiring coaches around the world, with many influenced by his philosophy 'Juego de Posicion.'

He has won eight championships, five big national cups, and two Champions leagues, in three different countries producing three legendary teams.

His side in Barcelona may be the biggest club team ever to have ever seen, though he's made a phenomenal achievement with his most recent success in Manchester City - winning back-to-back titles of 198 points.. Everyone knows that he's a tactical master and is well known in Cruyff's use of high-pressure possessive football that has reinvented the style of world soccer. But exactly what separates a Catalan from his time?

Although on a number of occasions Guardiola has confirmed that football cannot be played right or wrong, Guardiola does have a simple definition of what 'good football' means.

Some of the most fun types are the rapid counterattacking or build-up play with an emphasis on verticality. But for Pep, the focus is on intelligent opponents' exploitation.

Guardola strategies are very complicated with a detailed positioning instruction provided to each player to ensure that the shape of the team is perfect at all time. The basic concept behind playing football instead of counter-attacking pace is to retain a uniform form, to eventually become the final third to suffocate and overpower the opponents.

Guardiola divides the pitch into 24 areas, and demands that no two players occupy the same space. If the winger is on the outside, for example, the full-back has to dip in, and each player has to be aware of changes in the overall pattern. The concept must be always extended vertically and horizontally and give many 45° angles to whoever has the ball. This ultra-diligent grid structure produces endless triangles.

The players who occupy the channels between the center and the full back are the most important players in this grid, also known as the half-spaces.

Kevin De Bruyne and David Silva were operating jointly in City, and while other coaches exploiting that area more and more, no one has revealed this area's fertility as much as Guardiola. In the half-areas of Barcelona, Andres Iniesta and Lionel Messi danced and created a new tactical template that others followed. Guardian believes these areas are more productive than the central ten zone because players can view more of the pitch from a wider starting position and can open their bodies for a splitting defense pass.

In Manchester's first season, Pep only managed to reach the third position, with no silverware secure, in the Premier League. Many rival fans called him 'Fraudiola' and said his previous success was clearly due to his players' quality rather than to any advanced training technique. But twelve months later, City was crowned with a record-breaking 100 points. Football was worth waiting, with extremely effective daily wins and perfect team goals.

PART TWO

<u>KEVIN DE BRUYNE - *'GINGER PELE'*</u>

This is the complete story of the best nickname of the genius of football: 'Ginger Pele.' Our story about Kevin De Bruyne Childhood plus untold biographies provides you with a full account of important events since he was a child. Analysis includes his life story before fame, family life, and numerous facts about him, OFF and ON Pitch.

Yes, everybody knows that Kevin De Bruyne is one of the finest advanced players of modern day, although only a few know a great deal from outside the pitch about his life.

EARLY LIFE

Born by Herwig De Bruyne (father) and Anna De Bruyne, Kevin De Bruyne was born on 28 June 1991. (mother). He was born a White Caucasian, a minority of the white ethnic group in Belgium. He was a special child, one to be great when he was born.

Kevin has visited Ealing, England, his mom's family and Africa, where his mother comes originally, for the first part of his infancy. Another vacation was spent in Burundi and Ivory Coast, where the branches of his family were the oil company. The biggest oil investor in Africa, his grandfather (from his mother's side).

RISE TO FAME

Kevin started soccer in Drongen, Belgium, in his own city of Gent, at the age of four. He started the game well.

Since its very beginning the Belgian international increase has been meteoric. The first is hardwork and the second determination. This comes from two important characteristics. The first taste of stardom for Kevin De Bruyne came from his exemplary commitment to great heights. His hard work in his younger club was very successful and media attention in turn. Belgian football was seen as the future.

Belgium was tired of its old stock of players in this period because of its growing disadvantages. In football, they have never done well. They needed a grassroots football revolution. As a child who could spearhead such a child, Kevin was pointing. The wondrous boy was often faced with the media. He faced several sessions before and after his games.

The meteoric growth of the scouts in the Belgian youth football system has also been accompanied by curiosity.

He was wanted by every youth club. Kevin advanced quickly and became a favorite youth soccerist in the region

At 14, in the village of Drongen, outside Ghent, he left behind his life in his house. He entered the academy of Genk there and only saw his family on weekends. He learned to stay independent during this time. He made friends with a family who looked after him while there. Kevin was able to handle himself at 14 years of age.

He didn't earn a great deal of money, but handled what he had. "It was my parents who taught me how to run my self," Kevin said. *I'm not someone who in my life invests a lot of money. If I want to do something later, I save it for holidays – because we don't have much off time. I'm home during the season. Nice food, I cook myself. I am glad. I'm glad. When I was 14 years old, I lived alone."*

He left home to follow through with his career aspirations. When he made the decision, he was too young for you. It is actually a long way to go for Kevin in a short time. His grandmother cared for him so much. She's always visited him.

FAMILY LIFE

FATHER: Herwig De Bruyne's dad is in charge of the career of his

son.

Perfectly handling the affairs of his son off-pitch has strengthened

both sides. Herwig De Snr is a man who has successfully established

the master plan of his son's career as an intensive negotiator. This impacted his son, which resulted in him earning higher wages and improved sponsorship deals.

Herwig also warns against anyone who threatens his sons with respect to his football career.

Jose Mourinho was once warned by his disrespectful criticism of his son.

MOTHER: His mother is born from the UK, but was born in Burundi, East Africa where one of the petroleum companies of her family is based. This also means that their son's journey to Africa can be traced.

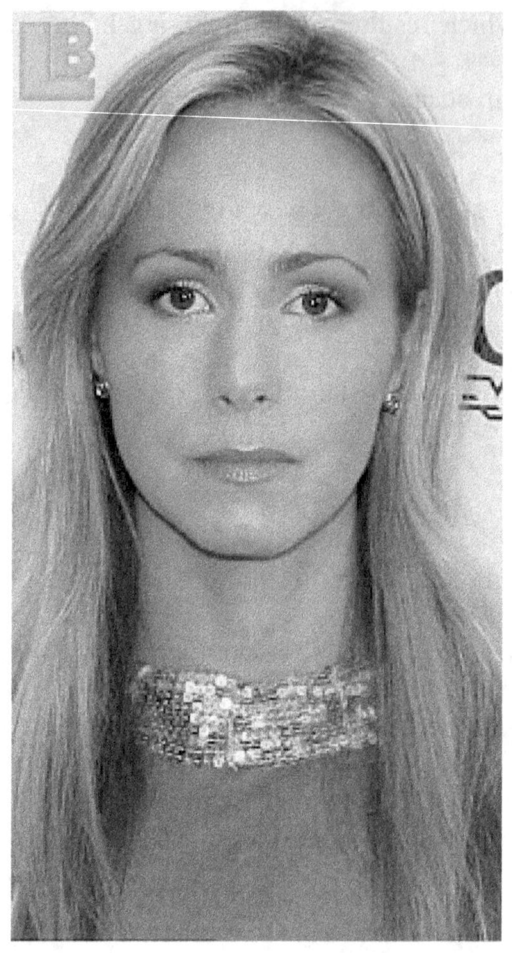

At 18 years of age, Anna De Bruyne born her soccer player's son. That's why she looks very young also. She is an oil engineering professional. She picked his father up and maintained his company both on the east and the ivory coasts of Burundi (West Africa).

She was mainly educated in a country in Eastern Africa before moving to Belgium where she met Kevin's father, Herwig De Bruyne Snr. and she fell in love with Kevin. The parents of Thou Anna De Bruyne live in Ealing Borough of London. This is where, as mentioned earlier, Kevin takes Christmas with his mother.

With regard to her son's encouragement, Anna De Bruyne often visits the stadiums much of its time to watch her son play football and support it. Following matches, Kevin rarely goes to the locker room. He finds time with his mother most of the time. Ideally, after every football match she gives him warm kisses.

SIBLING: He has a niece, who's Stefanie De Bruyne's name, too. She looks like her mother, while her father, her brother.

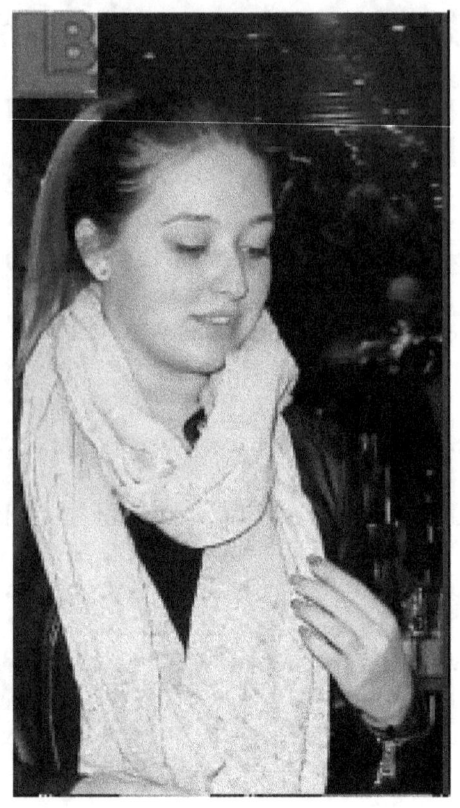

Relationship Life

Kevin De Bruyne is married at the time of writing to Michele Lacroix. She is undeniably quite stunning. The elegance and competence she is a paragon of. For a lot of reasons, Kevin loves her.

After the problems with his ex-girl friend, both parties met. They also met Thibaut Courtois, his best friend, who betrayed him by sleeping with his ex

Since its connection with Michele began Kevin has been a very happy guy. She was his best half. Michele is someone who made him the man he's always dreamed of being.

He left Chelsea to Wolfsburg, she was one of the reasons. Michele Lacroix was the lady that mended the broken heart of Kevin and healed his trauma that long haunted him.

He is never shy of publicly showing his love for her, particularly

before the crowd.

Mom's Kevin's friendship with her is completely endorsed. Both are

good friends and their son and friend have been watched and helped.

One of the reasons Kevin started his marriage plan with Michelle was because of her friendship. Kevin's only wanted a wife similar to his mother.

In 2016, Kevin De Bruyne was updated on her Instagram for the news of her engagement. In 2017, Michèle Lacroix married Kevin.

The Manchester City Star struggled for form in his club before his

marriage. His performance was very disturbed. His marriage to

Michele gave him a smile and contributed to a rapid return to shape.

The foreign partner of Belgium took his partner in a romantic break

in Paris after his marriage.

You, before your marriage, were blessed with a son, whom Mason

Milian De Bruyne was named.

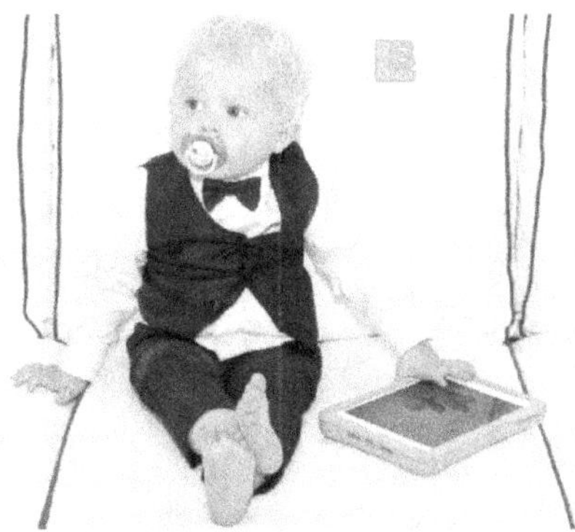

Kevin wants to have one of his son's picnic sessions. They like to go

without a shirt.

Aside from the bond of the father's son, every party was also seen

happy times.

Feud with Thibaut Courtois

Kevin was loved by Caroline Lijnen once. Thibaut Courtois, who was once considered a trusted friend of Kevin's, had been date for 3 years before their relationship was broken. The beginning of the feud was kindled by sleeping with his mother. The ex-girlfriend of the late Kevin de Bruyne Caroline Lijnen reveals that after Kevin had an affair with her former best friend he was cheated on with his best friend Thibaut Courtois..

Rumors about Lijnen's love triangle with Kevin initially started in April 2013 but now she has spoken and stated that she is intimate with Courtois, whom she met in Madrid, after De Bruyne confessed to adultery with her former best friend. She also remembered the best emotional treatment Courtois ever had, the sort of treatment de Bruyne could not receive.

"Thibaut Courtois gave me what you couldn't do in 3 years" in her word to Kevin...

She said that Kevin first stole, then paid back. She also said that her parents knew his cheats, but she couldn't do anything. Rather, perhaps because he is a star they sponsored their son.

Lijns said in her words...she said..."*I didn't say anything for months, as Kevin's parents said that if I gave my story, they would take legal action. I didn't tell anything. Kevin was proud to say he had my old best friend's affair. I gave him the choice. I gave him the choice. I was willing to give him another chance, but after that our relationship was never the same. I've been under pressure. I felt like I've been caged. I chose not to be quiet anymore. That's why I went to Thibaut for advice from his best friend. Thibaut comforted me and seized the occasion to reveal his feelings that he had concealed from me.*

He brought me what I hadn't got in three years with Kevin. I felt like a true woman. I will talk about it with Thibaut. He also had delicious meals made for me. It's never done to me by Kevin."

Meanwhile, after this incident, Courtois and de Bruyne have never patched their disagreements. This was one cause for Kevin to lose shape in Chelsea FC. De Bruyne was saddened by his best friend, Thibaut. He may have stayed for his place in Chelsea. Yet he couldn't afford his feelings. He left the club because of this and he came back as a rival. He mended his feelings through his friendship with Michele Lacroix.

<u>HIS THOUGHTS ON PREMIER LEAGUE</u>

In Kevin's words... "*The Premier League definitely is the best, but it's really hard for young people to get in. I don't see too many players playing abroad in English. The influence of our players in Belgium helps us. Perhaps it will also help England's players go abroad. The younger players are going to the [on loan] Championship. Perhaps it's easier to go to Germany's top league - that's very top. You will also hear a lot about good teams. Playing in Germany is even easier than playing the championship. I have even heard of English people living in England. If that's something, I don't know*

Maybe, he's got a point. Many talented football players from other European soccer nations came to England successfully. This has been an example in De Bruyne's narrative. In another country beside him he succeeded. He speaks fluent Dutch, French and English in three languages. He is pleased with the depth of his football experience.

WHY I LOVES LONDON

It is important to remember that Kevin is just 10 miles from Stamford Bridge, the grandfather's house in Ealing. He was there as a kid for Christmas.

In some Champions League matches of years ago, Kevin was part of the Genk Side. A special meeting was held in London before the match. They're gathering to watch him play the day. "I loved London that day, Kevin said. You have an English attitude in my mother, but I am fully Belgian. I was so much loved by the family because they wanted to converge for me. That's a big reason for me joining Chelsea FC. A club near the building"

FEUD WITH MOURINHO

Kevin began in 5 games for Chelsea, and from the 6th game he was benched. When he faced Mourinho, he wondered why he had been benched. Jose Mourinho, manager of Chelsea allegedly said, "Kevin, you do not train very well. Moreover, with your relationship issues, you are traumatized mentally. You have to build patience on the bank with your life. Get together and don't sit down on a bench."

That was a difficult answer to Kevin's contradictory questions from Jose Mourinho.

It was Kevin's father, Herwig De Bruyne also pushed hard demands for the first team for his son to play.

He also held several press conferences to discuss his son's lack of chances and his current interest in leaving the club. This led Jose Mourinho to respond again, and he said...

"I have been tired of the disruptions of Kevin De Bruyne. You have to make a decision if you have a player knocking at your door, crying every day he wants to leave. His dad forced his son into weeping into a crying infant. He was an agitated boy who was lost in shape, as his emotional life could not be handled"

Dad of De Bruyne, Herwig De Bruyne later defended a son as a reaction to Mourinho's tormented "cry boy..."

"Jose Mourinho is really bad about him because my son is a 'child upset.' He said that because he didn't play he decided to quit. It's not his emotional life. I think it should be a private matter for that part of him."

Finally Chelsea sold him in the Bundesliga for 18 million pounds to Wolfsburg.

PROVING CHELSEA WRONG

He scored 16 goals and 27 assists in a season when he played Wolfsburg. This helped him to become the outfield player of the 2015 Bundesliga. Afterwards he sought to return to the Premier League.

Usually Chelsea FC regretted having once sold it. That was Kevin's reaction to the Premier League.

"I'm a combatant. His Words... At Genk I learnt and at Wolfsburg I mastered it. Now I struggle for Premier League return. I will fight to cement my place at the first team in Manchester City. I am still going to fight to prove the wrong Chelsea FC." He really did that.

<u>**KDB Clothing Line**</u>

Kevin's own pop-up clothing business called 'KDB,' in conjunction with the Cult Eleven fashion label.

A part of the money is sent to the special Olympics from his line of clothes. In early 2014, Kevin was named Ambassador for the Special Olympics. In terms of financial support Kevin has much to thank in the 'Special Olympics' Committee.

Its goal is to help people with disabilities who have special sports facilities. Kevin invested more money to help them than any other sportsman did.

AT MANCHESTER CITY

In Premier League history books, another player from Manchester City encrypts his name. Today, Kevin De Bruyne gave me the chance to explore what is happening under these objectives.

The Belgian mid-camp player was Sheffield United's fifteenth assistant in the season, when he passed by Sergio Aguero, who broke the dead lock. Manchester City thus secured a 1-0 win in a game against Sheffield's deadly defence.

De Bruyne is also the first player to earn over 15 aids for 3 or more times a season. The Belgian has built a new bar for artistic quality.

KDB consistency has already exceeded all expectations. The player added to his previous playmaking achievements in the season, with 18 helps in 2016-17 and 16 helps in 2017-18. He would still have been blamed there, if he didn't do this for his injury in 2018-19.

The Belgian Playmaker has nevertheless achieved a milestone with no other players this season, with more than 15 games. Alexander-Arnold chasing him by nine assits is ahead of his compatriots.

He said: "These have been the wonderful things Kevin De Bruyne has discovered, and the revolution Sergio Aguero has done to any one of us in Europe and the rest of the world, this is a very good ending," said Blades boss Chris Wilder. He was very grateful for KDB.

There's no second thought about who is the best player in the region, and it would be incorrect to deny KDB as the best player in the year.

KEVIN DE BRUYNE: THE MODERN ATTACKING MIDFIELDER

Slowly, Kevin de Bruyne established himself both for his club and his country as a talisman. Had you told me this would have taken place after Chelsea sold him a few years ago for peanuts in Wolfsburg.

I honestly would have told you so much to stop playing football manager.

But how the Belgian mercurial tick and how Pep Guardiola's City of Manchester plays is so central to it. Now, this is what we will find out and we will make it easy for you to understand it as a reader.

Statistics:

Let's start by looking at de Bruyne statistically this season. The 19/20 Belgian played 28 league matches during the writing season, which led to eight goals and 16 premiere league assists.

Recently he told the athletic in an interview he fought for the support record for Thierry Henry and also talked to the Frenchman on an international level saying "I'm coming for you." It is difficult to see it that it does not split as the season continues on to remember how it worked in the last few years.

In your midfielder attack Kevin de Bruyne disappoints you all.

He not only makes good opportunities for his teammates, but shoots himself from risky situations.

Kevin De Bruyne's vast majority of his shots from central areas have been taken so far this season from the open air by Understat's shooting radar. 22 were taken from his left foot, 54 were taken from his right foot.

The points on the shot map indicate the shot quality. The greater the points the greater the shot's accuracy. The proof that he is a great long-distance shooter is shown by the targets of these low-resolution photos of admirable quality.

Statistically it can also be argued that Kevin de Bruyne was the 'full kit' in 19/20 as shown by the following radar:

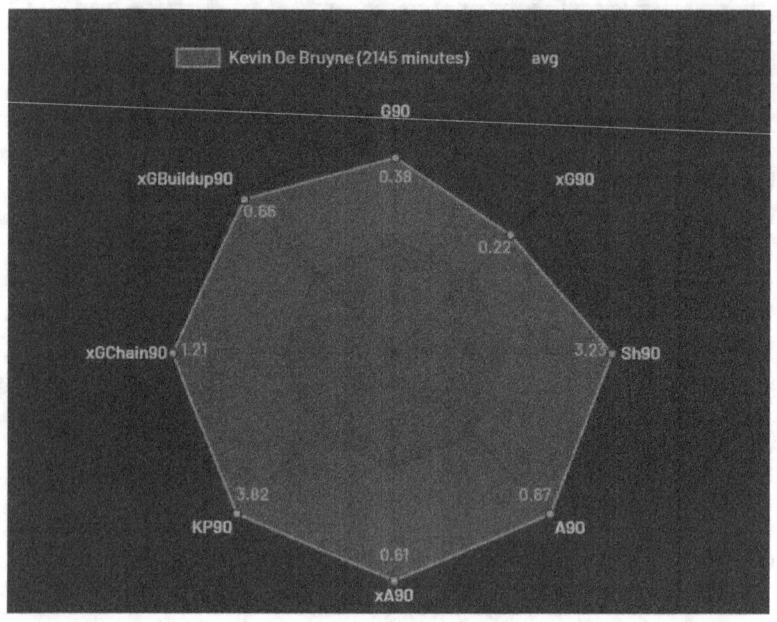

He has made excellent contributions in all stages of the game. For those who don't understand, the radar is read as follows

• Shot passes are approximately 3.82 per game • Shots targets are projected to be around 0.67 per game.

Ownership is 1,21 per game • Team building participation is 0,66 per game

• He contributes to the planned targets of 0.22 per game per 90

These are the signs of an offensive midfield with the right agility, tactical awareness, technical consistency and the potential to play many positions in one unit. This is not only a talisman but also a totally different one.

Now how he plays and what separates him from his colleagues

Style of Play:

You must get an understanding how Pep Guardiola is developing his Manchester city side in order to understand how Kevin de Bruyne plays. Every side of Pep has one feature, their football in nature is very robotic.

Each game will regularly display repetitive patterns on the pitch that allow an identity to build. In the city of Manchester, it was the fullbacks, because Guardiola inverted the city into dangerous situations, surges of widespread and central areas and of course, that allowed Kevin de Bruyne to shine.

His intellect is mostly distinct from me. He is the talisman of City, and yet anyone not Kante has problems in recognizing the Belgian Mercurial as he understands the game.

He would also carry his markers out wide so that Gundogan or Silva could attack the space left behind and would then join the attack himself.

This is seen in the screengrab above, with him either taking his marker or allowing Silva to occupy him widely. This provides de Bruyne with many options in dangerous conditions for teammates.

In the right half of the attack in Manchester City, the mercurial midfielder is typically found dominating their activities. Instead of the full-back, he normally would merge with the centerfloor on the right (Mahrez/Bernardo).

Below we present different radars on the pitch of the various

positions.

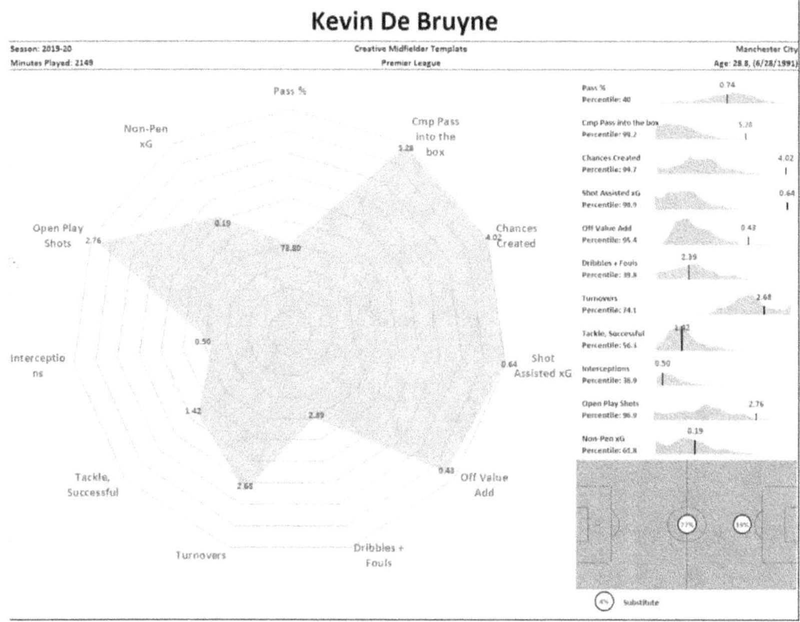

Kevin de Bruyne (Central Midfielder)

His Central Midfield radar shows his diverse tackling and the daily

strain he places on midfield opposition. However, despite the higher

defensive rates, he still generates 4.52 opportunities per game (!!!!)

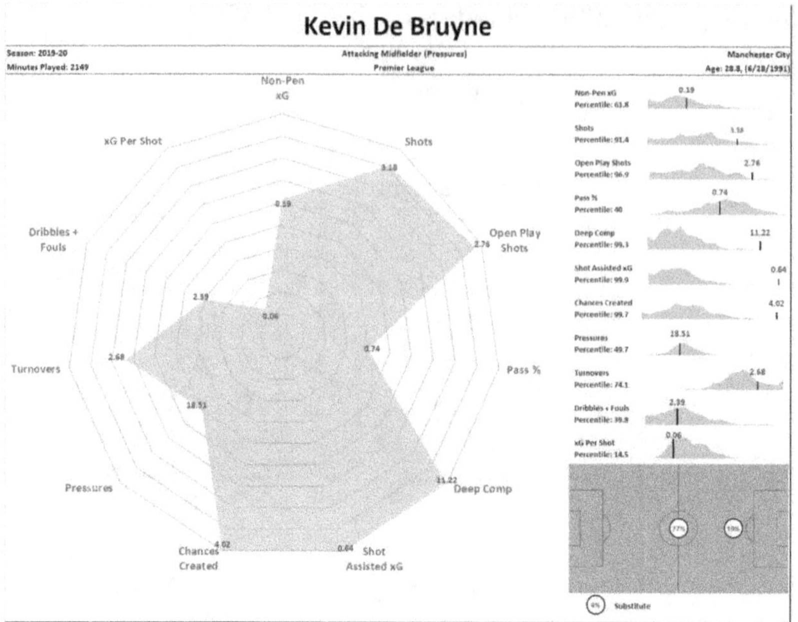

Kevin de Bruyne (Attacking Midfielder)

An offensive midfield player is very different, he plays ahead of the game and therefore less involved in the middle of the pitch leading to less attack per game. However, he only provides the same amount of opportunities and has far more goals

You can see that he can play various midfield roles inside the squad, whether it's a medium or forward-field (which he does for Belgia)

Since the League was unable to match Manchester City's technical consistency, Pep Guardiola deployed him as a central midfield player in a second in the Premier League, this was a mastermind when they won the two Premier League titles back in..

He was usually used as an advantage for Arsenal games because he was advised to push the ball through Arsenal's slight midfield makeup and to score a marvelous hat trick were not for the genius of Leno..

The 'Beckham' foot:

I'm going to leap to conclusions before you tell me... listen... Right foot is a rocket f*#king. At CrossBar, we mark KdB as the right foot of the beckham foot because of its capacity to cross the box or by-line and we say that such deliveries are not defensible.

See the following snap: See

The 'Beckham foot'

Bernardo Silva lets him ball and, in the KdB format, whips him in a nearly indefensible delivery.

The 'Beckham foot' 2

Sterling is not mistaken, and this has become a trademark of the midskate and you almost hope to benefit from the offer of one of his items when you watch him play.

It's what I like to call a hybrid, the norm nowadays of how you see an attacking medium-field. The #10 and #8 can be played concurrently in the same game by Kevin de Bruyne.

He drops deep to advance the game with Gundogan and Silva, but it is actually Crazy now, though still keepings an average 4.52 chances generated per game.

Manchester City hopes to be a fortress of global football, and it must maintain its precious asset for them to achieve these objectives.

But because the club is prohibited from the Champions League 2 years ago the core of the club is quoted as saying that if things do not change he possibly will look forward to a change.

The fans of Manchester will hope for a good result, while the rest of the league would most likely expect the reverse.

Manchester City's Record With And Without Kevin De Bruyne

Without Kevin De Bruyne the next few month or so, Manchester City will have to face up to the challenge of honours.

Due to a hamstring injury he sustained during the victory over Aston Villa De Bruyne was omitted during between the 4-6 weeks.

It's a huge blow to City as its initiative is gaining traction.

Pep Guardiolas men had played a total of 17 unbeatable games after losing 2-0 in Tottenham in November.

And they claimed their 10th consecutive victory following Saturday night's survival of a big FA Cup fright at Cheltenham Town, finally 3-1 win.

Pep Guardian describes the extent of the injury to Kevin De Bruyne

The competition is in the 5th round, as well as in the final round of the Carabao Cup and the final sixteen Champions League.

In the meantime, City is second at the Premier League, only a few points behind Manchester United champions – and a game in the side.

Guardian acknowledges that the absence of main man De Bruyne is hard to deal with, but has challenged his players to prove they can.

"You have to know I'll miss Kevin a lot and we'll miss him a lot, with the qualities that he has it he's almost irreplaceable.. In the Premier League last year, he was nominated for best, so we know what his goodness is, "The town boss said it.

"Yet at the same time you need something unforgettable when you want to obtain important titles: the charism and engagement which the team has in the locker room and the relationships between all the stars. "

When you respect each other you can't win titles. They're almost friends on and off the pitch, if not friends, to fight together.

"You can't win titles without this. Value wins games and more, but titles are won because the captains build and all accept this. You will win several matches in a row and titles if this happens." We will miss Kevin, we will wait for him as we waited for one year for Sergio (Aguero). Without Sergio almost a year ago we had an absolute legend, the best striker we had in our team, and one of the best strikers ever in the Premier League and without Sergio.

"A solution needs to be sought. We went to Stamford Bridge when we earned 3-1 in the first team of 14 players with too many injuries (Covid) and anything but the players were together and went ahead."
As a Manager and backroom staff we need to solve (Kevin) the many attributes he possesses which he can use and use the talents of the player in this role and to keep on playing and defending the dynamic.

"That is all we can do, we have done it in the past and we are going to do it in the future."

So, how have City fared with and without De Bruyne in the past?

Since arriving at the club in the summer of 2015, the Belgian midfielder has created 168 appearances within the Premier League.

He has <u>ended informed the winning facet in 116 of those</u>, whereas drawing twenty eight and losing 24.

That may be a win share of 69.05%, a loss percentage of 14.29% and works out as 2.23 points per game.

Manchester town consolidated their position at the highest of the league with a routine 3-0 convince Spurs on Saturday.

Without DE Bruyne, town have vie thirty six Premier League matches, winning 23, drawing four and losing 9

That is a slightly lower win percentage of 63.8%, figuring out at 2.02 points per game.

The increased loss percentage of 25% means City have suffered defeat in a quarter of their league fixtures without De Bruyne.

So, the team is statistically not as effective when he is not playing - but fans can take heart from the fact that the former Chelsea man did spend a decent chunk of the 2018-19 on the sidelines - and Guardiola's men went on to win the title as they edged out Liverpool in a dramatic race.

<u>**CONCLUSION**</u>

<u>**I'm Now A Complete Player**</u>

Kevin De Bruyne feels he has become "the complete player" and reveals his pride at being described as the best midfielder in the world. Though his Manchester City side have stumbled in the Premier League behind Liverpool, the Belgian was the current champions' outstanding performer before football was put on hold due to the coronavirus pandemic.

The injury issues of last year are currently firmly behind him. He has solely lost 3 Premier League games this season (2020/ 2021) and it's no coincidence that town lost them all. Speaking to Jamie Redknapp on The Football Show from his home while on lockdown, De Bruyne feels the consistency within his game has helped him become "a complete player". "It's difficult to comment on form but I'm the most complete player now," he said. "In every aspect of the game now I feel really comfortable. At Wolfsburg, I did incredibly well but I was more up and down but the past three seasons, maybe a little less last season, I'm happy as I'm playing at a constant level. "From the first game against West Ham to the last against Real Madrid, I've played really well. That makes it satisfying that I can be consistently good at a good enough level to perform." Jamie Carragher singled out De Bruyne for special praise earlier this season, describing him as "the best in the world" in his position while Redknapp has consistency called the midfielder the best passer in Premier League history and nominated him as his player of the season. De Bruyne's stats speak for themselves: he has four more assists, has created 21 more chances and seven more big chances than any other Premier League player. He also tops the Premier League charts for successful passes into the final third and successful crosses and corners. When asked regarding the controversy concerning his standing because the best within the world, American state Bruyne is happy his name is among the elite. "It feels me with pride," he said.

Kevin De Bruyne feels he has become "the complete player" and reveals his pride at being delineated because the best midfielder within the world. Though his Manchester town aspect have stumbled within the Premier League behind Liverpool, the Belgian was the current champions' outstanding performer before soccer was placed on hold because of the coronavirus pandemic. The injury problems with last year are presently firmly behind him. He has solely lost 3 Premier League games this season and it's no coincidence that city lost them all. Speaking to Jamie Redknapp on The soccer Show from his home whereas on lockdown, First State Bruyne feels the consistency among his game has helped him become "a complete player". "It's difficult to comment on form but I'm the most complete player now," he said. "In every aspect of the game now I feel really comfortable. At Wolfsburg, I did unbelievably well however i used to be a lot of up and down but the past three seasons, maybe a little less last season, I'm happy as I'm playing at a relentless level. "From the first game against West Ham to the last against Real Madrid, I've played really well. That makes it satisfying that I can be consistently good at a good enough level to perform."

Jamie Carragher singled out First State Bruyne for special praise earlier this season, describing him as "the best in the world" in his position while Redknapp has consistency known as the midfielder the simplest passer in Premier League history and appointed him as his player of the season. De Bruyne's stats speak for themselves: he has four more assists, has created twenty one a lot of possibilities and 7 more massive chances than the other Premier League player.

He conjointly cracks the Premier League charts for successful passes into the ultimate third and winning crosses and corners. When asked relating to the dispute regarding his standing as a result of the best among the world, state Bruyne is happy his name is among the elite.

"It feels me with pride," he said.

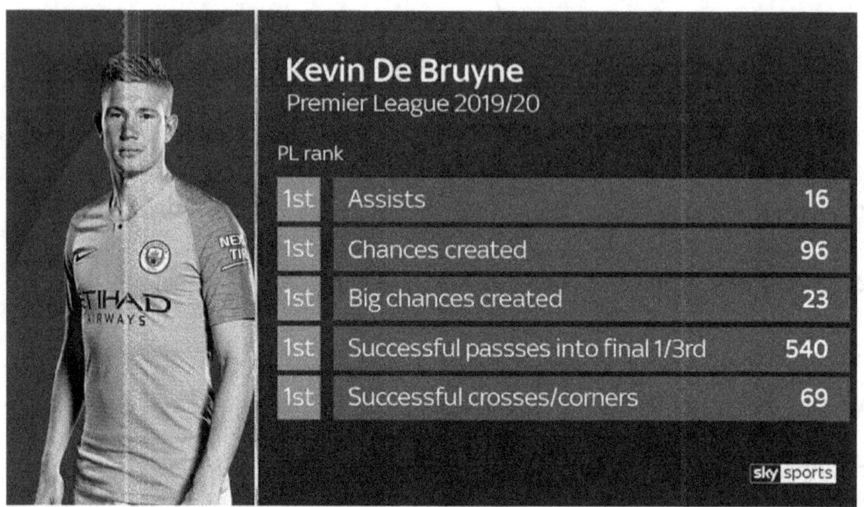

Kevin De Bruyne stats: 19/20 season

"It's difficult to debate form but I'm the foremost complete player

now," he said.

"In every aspect of the game now I feel really comfortable. At

Wolfsburg, I did implausibly well however i wont to be tons of up

and down but the past

three seasons, maybe slightly less last season, I'm happy as I'm

playing at a unbroken level.

"From the first game against West Ham to the last against Real Madrid,

I've played rather well . that creates it satisfying that I are often

consistently good at an honest enough level to perform."

Jamie Carragher singled out DE Bruyne for special praise earlier this

season, describing him as "the best within the world" in his position while

Redknapp has consistency referred to as the midfielder the only passer in

Premier League history and appointive him as his player of the season.

De Bruyne's stats represent themselves: he has four more assists, has

created twenty one tons of possibilities and seven more huge chances than the opposite

Premier League player. He conjointly first-rate the Premier League charts for

successful passes into the last word third and prospering crosses and corners.

When asked concerning the disputation regarding his standing as a result of the

best among the world, Bruyne is happy his name is among

the elite.

"It feels me proudly," he said.